The Spirit Behind the Sound

52 Devotionals for Worship Teams

Gerard Assey

The Spirit Behind the Sound:
52 Devotionals for Worship Teams
By
Gerard Assey

Published by:
Gerard Assey
19/18, Palli Arasan Street
Anna Nagar East
Chennai - 600 102

ISBN: 978-81-986974-0-0

Table of Contents

Introduction

Strengthening the Spirit Behind the Sound – A Year of Devotion for Worship Teams

Worship is not merely a sound. It is a **sacrifice**, a **surrender**, and a **spiritual posture** that rises from the depths of the heart. It is the fragrance of lives laid down in reverence to a holy God. The platform may amplify the music, but it is the *spirit behind the sound* that touches heaven.

In churches around the world, worship teams stand as frontline ministers—guiding congregations into the presence of God. Yet, amidst the responsibilities of rehearsals, schedules, chord charts, and Sunday logistics, it is easy to lose sight of the most critical part of our service: the heart. This book was birthed from that need—to re-center the heart of worship, one week at a time.

Why Weekly Devotionals?

These 52 devotionals have been prayerfully and thoughtfully written to equip, challenge, and disciple worship teams—from vocalists and musicians to sound engineers and creatives. Each devotional is more than just a weekly reflection; it's an invitation to go deeper in character, commitment, and spiritual maturity.

- ✓ They anchor the team in biblical truth before anchoring their in-ear monitors.
- ✓ They help the team grow in heart before growing in harmony.
- ✓ They develop worshipers, not just performers.

When the internal atmosphere of the worship team is healthy, the external expression of worship becomes powerful and pure.

How to Use This Book

Each of the 52 devotionals is designed to be used weekly—one for every week of the year. Worship leaders or team members can take turns leading the devotionals before rehearsal, during team meetings, or even on Sunday mornings. Here are a few suggestions to maximize impact:

- ✓ Set aside intentional time. Don't rush through it. Even 10–15 focused minutes can create powerful shifts.
- ✓ Encourage discussion. After the reflection, open up the floor for personal insights or testimonies. Let the team grow *together*.
- ✓ Take action. Every devotional includes a practical application. Commit as a team to follow through.
- ✓ Pray it in. End with a time of sincere prayer. Invite the Holy Spirit to seal the message.
- ✓ Rotate leadership. Allow different members to share the devotional. This builds ownership and spiritual confidence.

You can also:

- ✓ Use devotionals thematically (e.g., humility, service, unity)
- ✓ Customize devotionals around special worship nights or seasons
- ✓ Journal individual responses to the devotionals privately

The Benefits of Weekly Devotionals

Here's what regular spiritual nourishment can do for your worship team:

- ✓ Strengthens Spiritual Foundations
  Members aren't just showing up to sing—they're growing as disciples.
- ✓ Builds Unity in the Team
  Sharing the Word regularly creates deeper spiritual connection and trust.
- ✓ Re-aligns Focus on God
  Helps keep eyes on the *Giver*, not just the *gifts.*
- ✓ Develops Ministry Maturity
  Encourages repentance, surrender, servanthood, and a deeper understanding of true worship.
- ✓ Prepares the Heart Before the Sound
  Ensures the platform is filled with people who've already met God privately.

This Is More Than a Tool—It's a Calling

The goal of this devotional journey is not just musical excellence, but spiritual formation. Each week is an opportunity to tune our hearts to the frequency of heaven, so that our sound doesn't just fill a room—it moves the heart of God.

Worship leaders, this book is your companion as you shepherd your team beyond the stage and into the secret place, where worship begins. May this year be one of encounter, transformation, and divine intimacy. And may every note you play and every word you sing be saturated with the Spirit of the living God.

Let's raise more than a sound—let's raise a sacrifice.

"But the hour is coming, and now is, when the true worshipers will worship the Father in spirit and truth; for the Father is seeking such to worship Him." — John 4:23 (NKJV)

Devotional 1:
Worship Beyond the Stage

Scripture: *John 4:23-24 (NIV)- "Yet a time is coming and has now come when the true worshipers will worship the Father in the Spirit and in truth, for they are the kind of worshipers the Father seeks. God is spirit, and his worshipers must worship in the Spirit and in truth."*

Reflection:
Worship is not confined to the sound system, the setlist, or the platform. It's not something we do only during rehearsals or Sunday services. Jesus' words here redefine worship. He's not looking for performance. He's looking for *truth*—real hearts aligned with the Holy Spirit.
As worship team members, it's easy to associate our offering to God with how well we sing or play. But God doesn't look at how perfectly we hit the harmonies or whether the transitions are seamless. He looks at our hearts. Are we worshiping to be seen? Or are we worshiping because we're in awe of who He is?
Worship in spirit means it flows from the depth of your being, not just your vocal cords or fingers. Worship in truth means it is anchored in Scripture, in honesty, and in a real relationship with God—not a show.

Challenge:
Before you touch your instrument, warm up your voice, or sing your first note this week—ask yourself:

- ✓ *"Am I worshiping in Spirit and in Truth—or am I going through the motions?"*

- ✓ Have you gotten so caught up in technical excellence that you've forgotten spiritual intimacy? Have you been more focused on *how* you sound than *why* you worship?

Application:

- ✓ Daily Worship: Commit to 10 minutes of personal worship every day this week. No mic. No audience. Just you and Jesus. Sing, pray, or sit in stillness.
- ✓ Heart Check-In: Before each rehearsal/service, pause and pray this: *"Lord, purify my motives. Let my worship be in Spirit and in Truth."*
- ✓ Team Discussion: Ask each team member next practice: *"What does worship in Spirit and Truth look like in your life right now?"* Listen without judgment.

Devotional 2:
The Heart Before the Sound

Scripture: *1 Samuel 16:7 (NIV)- "The Lord does not look at the things people look at. People look at the outward appearance, but the Lord looks at the heart."*

Reflection:

We spend hours fine-tuning our vocals and learning chords. But how much time do we spend tuning our hearts? In this passage, God reminds Samuel that what impresses man is not what impresses Him. A flawless performance means little if it's coming from a heart disconnected from God.

Worship begins in the heart, not the mic. We can sing "Holy Spirit, you are welcome here," but if our hearts are harboring pride, bitterness, or competition, we block the very presence we're inviting.

Challenge:

Examine your heart this week. Is there something that GOD detests that you are hiding? Is there pride in your gifting? Are you comparing yourself to someone else on the team?

Application:

- ✓ Spend time in prayer before practice and ask God to search your heart (Psalm 139:23-24).
- ✓ Take a few moments as a team to repent silently before starting rehearsal.
- ✓ Choose to affirm another teammate this week, especially one you tend to compare yourself to.

Devotional 3:
When Excellence Becomes Idolatry

Scripture: *Colossians 3:23 (NIV) -"Whatever you do, work at it with all your heart, as working for the Lord, not for human masters."*

Reflection:
Excellence is important—but when excellence becomes the goal instead of worship, we're out of alignment. We rehearse, plan, and perfect... but if it becomes about the *sound* over the *Savior*, it becomes idolatry.

We are called to bring our best to the Lord, not for applause, likes, or recognition. A heart of worship doesn't pursue perfection to impress man—it gives its best to honor God.

Challenge:
Do you find your mood or self-worth rising and falling with how well practice goes? Are you driven more by fear of mistakes than desire to glorify God?

Application:

- ✓ Shift your "why" this week: Remind yourself before every song, "I'm doing this for Him."
- ✓ Replace performance pressure with presence focus. Invite God to take center stage—literally and spiritually.
- ✓ Share with the team: What is one area you've been more performance-driven than Spirit-led?

Devotional 4:
The Silent Worshiper

Scripture: *Psalm 46:10 (NIV)- "Be still, and know that I am God."*

Reflection:
Worship is not always loud. Not always musical. Sometimes, worship is *stillness*. As worshipers, we can mistake noise for power. But God often speaks most clearly in the silence.
Stillness teaches us trust. It reminds us that worship isn't only what we give vocally—it's also how we posture our hearts quietly before Him. Some of the most powerful moments happen when the music stops.

Challenge:
Have you been afraid of silence in worship? Do you fill every moment with music out of discomfort or habit?

Application:

- ✓ Build intentional silence into your personal worship this week.
- ✓ During team worship, pause for 1-2 minutes of total stillness. Invite the Holy Spirit to speak.
- ✓ Reflect and journal what God revealed in the quiet.

Devotional 5:
The Attitude of Gratitude

Scripture: *Psalm 100:4 (NIV)- "Enter his gates with thanksgiving and his courts with praise; give thanks to him and praise his name."*

Reflection:

Thanksgiving is not optional in worship—it's the gateway. It's how we enter His presence. Gratitude softens our hearts, tunes our spirits, and aligns us with Heaven. When we lose thankfulness, worship becomes a routine instead of a relationship.

Even when things go wrong on stage—wrong chord, wrong note, wrong key—gratitude resets our focus from frustration to God's goodness.

Challenge:

Has your heart been more focused on what's *not right*—in your voice, your team, or your church—than what's *already good*?

Application:

- ✓ Begin every rehearsal with a "gratitude circle"—each member shares one thing they're thankful for.
- ✓ Create a running list of "Worship Wins"—times God moved, however small. Celebrate them.
- ✓ In personal worship, write a psalm of thanksgiving to God.

Devotional 6:
One Sound, One Spirit

Scripture: *Romans 15:5-6 (NIV) -"...so that with one mind and one voice you may glorify the God and Father of our Lord Jesus Christ."*

Reflection:

Musically, harmony is beautiful—but spiritually, unity is essential. God is not impressed by tight harmonies if there's tension among the team.

Unity multiplies anointing. Division kills momentum. When we worship with "one voice" in spirit—not just vocally—we release a powerful, unified sound that invites heaven to touch earth.

Challenge:

Are there unspoken offenses or unresolved tensions in the team? Are you carrying offense while lifting your hands?

Application:

- ✓ Take time to reconcile if needed. Forgive, even if unspoken.
- ✓ Pray for unity before every set—not just for sound, but spirit.
- ✓ Practice *spiritual harmony*—celebrate differences, serve one another, and stay on mission.

Devotional 7:
Worship Is Warfare

Scripture: *2 Chronicles 20:21-22 (NIV)- "...As they began to sing and praise, the Lord set ambushes against their enemies..."*

Reflection:
When Jehoshaphat's army faced overwhelming odds, they didn't start with swords—they started with song. Worship *shifted* the battle.
Your worship isn't background music—it's front-line warfare. When you sing, walls fall. Chains break. Demons flee. Whether you feel it or not, heaven responds when faith-filled praise goes up.

Challenge:
Have you been passive in worship lately—forgetting the authority you carry in your praise?

Application:

- ✓ Speak truth in your worship. Declare God's promises aloud.
- ✓ As a team, identify one area of spiritual opposition and declare worship over it this week.
- ✓ Don't hold back. Sing like you're leading an army—because you are.

Devotional 8:
From Stage to Secret Place

Scripture: *Matthew 6:6 (NIV) -"But when you pray, go into your room, close the door and pray to your Father, who is unseen..."*

Reflection:
Public worship must overflow from private devotion. You cannot give what you haven't received. The secret place is where your voice is strengthened, your heart is refined, and your intimacy deepens.
The more time you spend in the secret place, the more powerful your worship becomes on the stage. Without the secret place, you're just performing.

Challenge:
Has your private worship life been weak? Are you depending on rehearsals to fill what only solitude can?

Application:

- ✓ Schedule three "secret place sessions" this week—just you and God. No agenda.
- ✓ Share in pairs next week: What did God reveal in your personal time with Him?
- ✓ Make "private before public" your worship motto.

Devotional 9:
Carriers of His Presence

Scripture: *2 Samuel 6:14 (NIV)- "Wearing a linen ephod, David was dancing before the Lord with all his might."*

Reflection:

David didn't just play music—he *hosted* the presence of God. When the Ark of the Covenant returned, he danced with *all his might* before the Lord. No image. No restraint. No concern for public opinion. Why? Because David wasn't performing. He was hosting the presence of a holy God.

Worship leaders and team members aren't entertainers. We are *carriers* of the presence. Our job is not just to lead songs—it's to create a space where God is welcome to dwell.

But we can't carry His presence on Sunday if we haven't cultivated His presence Monday through Saturday. God doesn't rest on gifting; He rests on hunger and holiness.

Challenge:

Are you worshiping like David—with undignified, passionate surrender? Or have you become polished, but distant?

Application:

- ✓ Ask the Lord to renew a hunger for His presence.
- ✓ During rehearsal, pause to *minister to the Lord* before focusing on any song.
- ✓ Encourage team members to spend personal time "hosting" God at home this week.

Devotional 10: Worship Without Rival

Scripture: *Exodus 20:3 (NIV) -"You shall have no other gods before me."*

Reflection:

God doesn't compete for attention—He demands it. Worship without rival means He has no competition in your heart. Not ministry. Not music. Not your gifting. Not even the worship itself.

We can sometimes idolize the act of worship more than the One we worship. When the platform becomes the source of our identity, we've misplaced our affection. God isn't interested in being part of your life—He wants to be Lord of it.

Challenge:

Has worship become something you do to feel good? Has your identity become too tied to the role you play rather than the God you serve?

Application:

- ✓ Lay your gifting on the altar this week in prayer. Say, "God, even this is yours."
- ✓ Reflect: What would your worship look like if no one ever saw or applauded you again?
- ✓ Ask the Lord to purify your desires—to want *Him more than anything else*.

Devotional 11:
The Sound of Obedience

Scripture: *1 Samuel 15:22 (NIV)- "To obey is better than sacrifice, and to heed is better than the fat of rams."*

Reflection:

Saul lost God's favor not because he didn't worship—but because he disobeyed. God equates obedience with true worship. Your sound can be beautiful, but if it's not built on obedience, it's noise.

Obedience tunes your spirit. Every time you say "yes" to God—even when it's inconvenient—you make music that pleases Him. And disobedience—no matter how skilled you are—eventually creates spiritual dissonance.

Challenge:

Is there something God has asked you to do (or stop doing) that you've been ignoring? Have you been singing louder than you're obeying?

Application:

- ✓ Ask God to reveal any area where obedience is lacking.
- ✓ Make a list of "delayed obediences" and start acting on them.
- ✓ Remind your team: Obedience is the clearest sound of worship heaven hears.

Devotional 12:
The Posture of Surrender

Scripture: *Romans 12:1 (NIV)- "Offer your bodies as a living sacrifice, holy and pleasing to God—this is your true and proper worship."*

Reflection:
Worship is more than music—it's offering your *entire life* to God. The stage isn't the altar. *You are.* Your attitude, your thought life, your schedule, your relationships—everything is an act of worship when surrendered.
God doesn't want just your voice; He wants your life. Worship isn't defined by how loud you sing, but how low you bow—how yielded your heart is to His will, His timing, His process.

Challenge:
Have you separated your "worship life" from your "real life"? Is there an area you've been unwilling to surrender?

Application:

- ✓ Spend time asking: "God, what area of my life do You want on the altar?"
- ✓ As a team, pray: "Lord, we place our entire lives as living sacrifices. Use us however You will."
- ✓ Choose one practical act of surrender this week—time, energy, plans.

Devotional 13:
Leading From the Overflow

Scripture: *Luke 6:45 (NIV) -"For the mouth speaks what the heart is full of."*

Reflection:
We don't just lead with our voices—we lead with our spirit. What flows from you on the platform is what you've allowed to fill you off it. If your heart is full of peace, love, and truth, that will pour out in worship. If it's full of pride, anxiety, or frustration—that leaks, too.
We must be so filled with the presence of God that our ministry is simply the *overflow*. Don't strive to lead from empty. Lead from *fullness.*

Challenge:
Are you leading from overflow—or burnout? Are you trying to draw water from a dry well?

Application:

- ✓ Prioritize spiritual filling—prayer, the Word, rest.
- ✓ Before each rehearsal, ask: "What's filling me right now?"
- ✓ Create space for the team to "fill up" spiritually before leading others.

Devotional 14:
An Audience of One

Scripture: *Matthew 6:1 (NIV)- "Be careful not to practice your righteousness in front of others to be seen by them..."*

Reflection:
When we lead worship, there are people in front of us—but only One we're truly singing for. The temptation to impress, perform, or gain approval is strong. But worship isn't a concert. It's communion.
When we shift our focus from the crowd to Christ, our posture changes. Our priorities change. Our pressure disappears—because when it's for God, we don't need to perform. We just need to *be real*.

Challenge:
Are you more focused on *how people perceive you* than on God's pleasure?

Application:

- ✓ Begin every set with this prayer: "God, this is all for You. Let it please You alone."
- ✓ Ask: "If no one claps or compliments me today, will I still feel fulfilled?"
- ✓ Encourage the team to lead as if God is the only one in the room—because, spiritually, He is.

Devotional 15:
When the Song is Hard to Sing

Scripture: *Habakkuk 3:17–18 (NIV) -"Though the fig tree does not bud... yet I will rejoice in the Lord, I will be joyful in God my Savior."*

Reflection:

Not every week is easy. There are Sundays you'll lead while hurting, grieving, or feeling spiritually dry. But real worship doesn't come from ease—it often comes from sacrifice.

Habakkuk praised even when everything fell apart. That's mature worship—singing when your heart is heavy, trusting when life is hard, declaring God's goodness when circumstances are unclear. God treasures those songs. They cost something.

Challenge:

Have you been going through the motions while quietly struggling? Are you afraid to worship honestly in your pain?

Application:

- ✓ Be vulnerable before God. Tell Him the truth. Worship from *that place*.
- ✓ Create a moment of lament or honest expression in worship—God can handle it.
- ✓ Encourage team members: *It's okay to worship with tears. Heaven hears them as praise.*

Devotional 16: The Ministry of Preparation

Scripture: *Proverbs 21:31 (NIV)- "The horse is made ready for the day of battle, but victory rests with the Lord."*

Reflection:

Many worship teams wait until the stage to engage spiritually. But preparation is *ministry*, not just a practical step. Rehearsing songs is good—but preparing our hearts is even better. The difference between a worship set that moves people and one that simply sounds good often lies in what happened before the service.

David didn't walk into Goliath's battle unprepared—he had trained with the lion and the bear. Likewise, private preparation (spiritually and musically) is what empowers us for public ministry.

Challenge:

Do you show up to serve spiritually ready—or only musically familiar? Are you preparing your heart or just your instrument?

Application:

- ✓ Spend 10 quiet minutes with the Lord before rehearsals.
- ✓ Encourage your team to prepare spiritually throughout the week—not just on service day.
- ✓ Set the tone: Practice is worship. Get there early, stay prayerful.

Devotional 17:
Excellence Without Perfectionism

Scripture: *Colossians 3:23 (NIV)- "Whatever you do, work at it with all your heart, as working for the Lord, not for human masters."*

Reflection:

There's a fine line between excellence and perfectionism. Excellence honors God. Perfectionism tries to *be* God. One flows from devotion; the other from insecurity or pride.

God deserves our best—but He doesn't demand flawlessness. When we pursue excellence in our sound, teamwork, or flow, we're worshiping. But when we get frustrated, controlling, or critical when things aren't perfect, we've made it about us. God is moved by faithfulness, not flawlessness.

Challenge:

Are you pursuing excellence to glorify God—or perfection to impress others?

Application:

- ✓ As a team, define what "excellence" means biblically.
- ✓ Create space to make mistakes without shame—encourage growth, not guilt.
- ✓ Celebrate effort and growth as worship unto the Lord.

Devotional 18:
The Power of Silent Worship

Scripture: *Psalm 46:10 (NIV) -"Be still, and know that I am God."*

Reflection:
In a world of noise—and on a team full of sound—it's easy to forget the power of silence in worship. But silence can be just as holy, just as moving, as music. True worship isn't just sound—it's stillness, reverence, awe.
Sometimes, we fill the space because silence feels uncomfortable. But God often speaks in the silence. If our worship is always loud, we may miss His whisper.

Challenge:
Are you uncomfortable in God's silence? Are you allowing moments of stillness to be part of your worship?

Application:

- ✓ Build intentional moments of silence or pause into worship sets.
- ✓ Personally practice "still worship" at home—just you and God, no music.
- ✓ Reflect: "Is my heart still noisy, even when the music stops?"

Devotional 19:
Staying Spiritually Fit

Scripture: *1 Timothy 4:7b–8 (NIV)- "Train yourself to be godly. For physical training is of some value, but godliness has value for all things."*

Reflection:
Just as musicians rehearse and vocalists warm up, our spiritual lives require *training*. No one becomes godly by accident. Being part of a worship team means you're in spiritual leadership—and leaders can't afford to be spiritually lazy.
The truth is: the spiritual condition of a worship leader *leaks*. If you're weak spiritually, it will show in your worship, your attitude, your responses.

Challenge:
Are you spiritually fit—or spiritually flabby? Are you training in godliness the same way you train musically?

Application:

- ✓ Set a weekly personal rhythm of Word, worship, and prayer.
- ✓ As a team, check in: "How are we growing spiritually this month?"
- ✓ Memorize a Scripture together each week. Keep your "spiritual muscles" strong.

Devotional 20:
Protecting the Unity

Scripture: *Ephesians 4:3 (NLT)- "Make every effort to keep yourselves united in the Spirit, binding yourselves together with peace."*

Reflection:

A divided worship team can never lead people into the presence of a united God. Unity is not automatic—it's something we protect. The enemy often attacks worship teams with gossip, comparison, and offense because a united team carries power.

God anoints unity (Psalm 133). Worship becomes powerful when hearts are connected, not just voices.

Challenge:

Have you allowed offense, jealousy, or comparison to build walls in your team?

Application:

- ✓ Have open, honest conversations with love when tension arises.
- ✓ Make space for team check-ins—not just about music, but about hearts.
- ✓ Before practice or service, pause to pray for unity. Always.

Devotional 21:
The Sacred Sound

Scripture: *Exodus 28:35* — "Aaron must wear it when he ministers... so that the sound of it will be heard when he enters the Holy Place before the Lord..."

Reflection:
Aaron's garments made *sound* as he entered the holy place. It wasn't noise—it was *sacred sound*. Worship is more than melodies—it is movement into holiness. God is not just listening to our notes; He's listening for our *spiritual resonance*. Is our sound shaped by the Spirit or by style? Sacred sound carries reverence. It's not about loud or soft, modern or traditional—it's about whether God hears worship that comes from a consecrated heart. Our worship must *announce holiness*, not just excellence. Let your sound be sacred—not just skilled.

Challenge:
Is your worship set apart—or just well-produced?
Application:

- ✓ Before each set, pray: "Let our sound be holy, not just harmonious." Dedicate every note, every transition, every song to God afresh

---

Devotional 22: Worship in the Weary

Scripture: *Isaiah 40:31* — "But those who hope in the Lord will renew their strength..."

Reflection:

Ministry can drain you. Late nights, rehearsals, pouring out—it's easy to feel burned out. But Isaiah promises strength to those who hope—not just work—in the Lord. Worshipers must learn the rhythm of **rest and reliance**. You cannot pour from an empty cup. Some of the best worship sets are not born out of hustle, but of *hope*. God never asked us to do this in our own strength. He renews those who wait on Him. Let your energy come from intimacy, not effort. When we worship out of overflow, we stop striving and start soaring.

Challenge:

Are you running on fumes or on faith?

Application:

- ✓ Take one evening this week to *rest* in God's presence without prepping a setlist. Just be. Let God refill what you've been pouring out.

Devotional 23:
The Power of Consistency

Scripture: *Luke 16:10 (NIV) -"Whoever can be trusted with very little can also be trusted with much..."*

Reflection:

God honors *consistency* more than occasional intensity. It's not about leading worship once with fire—it's about leading faithfully week after week, whether you feel it or not.

Some weeks you'll be tired. Some weeks it will feel mundane. But when you're consistent, you're building a testimony of trust. God notices the ones who show up, pour out, and keep going.

Challenge:

Have you treated consistency as ordinary? Are you showing up in both big and small moments?

Application:

- ✓ Reflect: Am I showing up faithfully even when it's inconvenient?
- ✓ Celebrate consistent team members. Thank them for staying the course.
- ✓ Ask God to give you fresh strength to keep serving with joy—again and again.

Devotional 24:
From Talent to Anointing

Scripture: *Acts 4:13 (NIV) -"They were astonished... they took note that these men had been with Jesus."*

Reflection:

Talent impresses. Anointing transforms. In Acts, the disciples didn't have degrees or training—but they had *been with Jesus.* That was their power. As worship leaders, talent can get us applause—but only anointing breaks yokes.

Anointing doesn't come from skill—it comes from *closeness* with God. It's the residue of intimacy. When you spend time with Jesus, it shows. People may not be able to describe it—but they'll know something's different.

Challenge:

Are you depending more on talent than time with Jesus?

Application:

- ✓ Increase your private time with God. Let your public ministry flow from it.
- ✓ Ask: "Would there still be power in my worship if I lost my voice today?"
- ✓ Seek anointing over applause. Let the fragrance of your intimacy linger on the stage.

Devotional 25:
The Weight of the Platform

Scripture: *James 3:1 (NIV)- "Not many of you should become teachers, my fellow believers, because you know that we who teach will be judged more strictly."*

Reflection:
The platform is not just a stage—it's a place of spiritual responsibility. Leading worship is a form of leadership, and with that comes weight. What we model on stage—our attitude, reverence, and even body language—shapes how others approach God.
It's easy to take the mic lightly. But when you realize you're not just singing songs—you're representing God's heart—it humbles you. The fear of the Lord must stay central.

Challenge:
Do you carry the platform lightly or with holy reverence?

Application:

- ✓ Reflect before every service: *"What am I communicating about God today?"*
- ✓ Stay accountable in lifestyle, speech, and character.
- ✓ Don't just prepare the music—prepare your heart for leadership.

Devotional 26:
Worship Beyond Emotion

Scripture: *Hebrews 13:15 (NIV) -"Through Jesus, therefore, let us continually offer to God a sacrifice of praise..."*

Reflection:
Worship is often emotional—but it's not built *on* emotion. There are Sundays we don't "feel" it—and that's okay. True worship is a sacrifice. It's choosing to honor God when you're exhausted, burdened, or numb.
God receives praise not because it's perfect, but because it's offered in surrender. Feelings come and go. Faithful worship is not dependent on moods.

Challenge:
Are you only worshiping when you "feel" it?

Application:

- ✓ Choose to lead with your spirit, not your emotions.
- ✓ During tough weeks, remind your team: *"This is a sacrifice of praise."*
- ✓ Let your faith lead your feelings, not the other way around.

Devotional 27: Dealing with Disappointment in Ministry

Scripture: *Psalm 42:11 (NIV)- "Why, my soul, are you downcast? Why so disturbed within me? Put your hope in God..."*

Reflection:

Worship ministry comes with seasons of discouragement—low attendance, technical issues, personal burnout, or even lack of response from the congregation. It's easy to internalize that and become weary.

But David shows us how to talk to our souls. He reminds himself that hope is not in circumstances, but in God. Our calling isn't validated by applause—it's validated by obedience.

Challenge:

Have you let discouragement dim your joy in serving?

Application:

- ✓ Be honest with God about disappointments. He can handle it.
- ✓ Speak truth to your soul: *God is still worthy.*
- ✓ Reconnect with your "why"—you're doing this for Him, not for results.

Devotional 28: Taming the Tongue on the Team

Scripture: *Ephesians 4:29 (NIV) -"Do not let any unwholesome talk come out of your mouths, but only what is helpful for building others up..."*

Reflection:

Every worship team fights the silent battle of words—sarcasm, gossip, criticism, backbiting. These things poison the spiritual atmosphere faster than off-key notes.

God cares deeply about how we speak to and about one another. A team that *builds* each other becomes a team God can use mightily. Our mouths must match our message.

Challenge:

Are your words on the team building up or breaking down?

Application:

- ✓ Set a team culture of speaking life—no gossip, no negativity.
- ✓ Pause before you joke or criticize: *"Is this helpful?"*
- ✓ Encourage at least one team member intentionally each week.

Devotional 29:
No Room for Ego

Scripture: *John 3:30 (NIV) -"He must become greater; I must become less."*

Reflection:

Worship leaders face a unique temptation—applause. Even when we say it's "all about Jesus," it's easy to enjoy the attention. Pride is subtle, and ego can creep in disguised as excellence.

John the Baptist had the perfect response to growing popularity—"I must decrease." That's the cry of every true worshiper. The stage is not for self-promotion. It's for Jesus alone.

Challenge:

Have you craved recognition more than revelation?

Application:

- ✓ Guard your heart after services—are you seeking feedback or God's pleasure?
- ✓ Celebrate unseen roles (sound, lyrics, backup) just as much as vocalists.
- ✓ Regularly pray: *"Jesus, increase. I decrease."*

Devotional 30:
Keep the Fire Burning

Scripture: *Leviticus 6:13 (NIV)- "The fire must be kept burning on the altar continuously; it must not go out."*

Reflection:

In the Old Testament, the fire on the altar was never to go out. Likewise, the fire of worship in our hearts needs constant fueling. Passion is not automatic—it requires intentional pursuit.

Sometimes we confuse spiritual dryness with burnout—but it's often just spiritual neglect. The more we neglect personal time with God, the colder the fire becomes.

Challenge:

Is your worship fire burning low due to spiritual neglect?

Application:

- ✓ Rekindle your fire through daily devotion, not just rehearsals.
- ✓ Schedule time alone with God *just to worship*—no agenda.
- ✓ Create a "fire check" habit as a team. Ask: *"Where's your flame this week?"*

Devotional 31:
Character Over Charisma

Scripture: *Titus 2:7-8 (NIV)- "In everything set them an example by doing what is good..."*

Reflection:
Talent can get us places, but only character keeps us there. In worship ministry, charisma may attract people, but it's integrity that pleases God. He's not just watching your stage presence—He's watching your *life*.
People are watching how you live off-stage. Is your walk consistent with your worship?

Challenge:
Does your lifestyle support or contradict your platform presence?

Application:

- ✓ Make time for accountability relationships.
- ✓ Focus on fruit, not just gifting.
- ✓ Regularly invite God to inspect your life: *"Search me, O God."*

Devotional 32:
What Are You Tuning To?

Scripture: *Romans 12:2 (NIV) -"Do not conform to the pattern of this world, but be transformed by the renewing of your mind..."*

Reflection:

Musicians know that tuning an instrument is crucial—but what you tune to matters. If you're tuning to the wrong standard, you'll be out of sync. The world has a pitch: popularity, perfection, performance. God has His own pitch: surrender, humility, holiness.

You can't lead people into God's presence if you've tuned your heart to the wrong frequency.

Challenge:

Are you more tuned to culture, comparison, or Christ?

Application:

- ✓ Ask before every set: *"What am I tuning to this week?"*
- ✓ Saturate yourself in God's Word to stay tuned to His truth.
- ✓ Let worship be a moment to re-align hearts—not just hit right notes.

Devotional 33:
Following the Cloud, Not the Crowd

Scripture: *Exodus 40:36-37 (NIV)- "In all the travels of the Israelites, whenever the cloud lifted... they set out... but if the cloud did not lift, they did not set out..."*

Reflection:

The Israelites followed the *cloud of God's presence*, not their own agenda. In worship leading, we often plan well—but God sometimes moves differently. Worship is not about performing a setlist—it's about following the Spirit.

We must learn to be sensitive to God's movement—not just people's reactions. Sometimes, the crowd may want one thing, but the cloud of God is moving somewhere else.

Challenge:

Are you more focused on pleasing people or following God's presence?

Application:

- ✓ Pray: *"Lord, help me follow You, not just my plan."*
- ✓ Build flexibility into your team culture.
- ✓ Be bold to pause, linger, or shift as God leads—even if it costs "flow."

Devotional 34: Worship as a Response, Not a Requirement

Scripture: *1 John 4:19 (NIV)- "We love because he first loved us."*

Reflection:

Worship is not something we *initiate*—it's a response to God's love. We don't lead worship to earn His presence—we worship because we already *have* it. Grace is the fuel of true praise.

If we forget this, worship becomes pressure, not passion. God loved us first. Our songs, our service, our sounds are just grateful replies to divine mercy.

Challenge:

Are you worshiping as a duty—or a delight flowing from grace?

Application:

- ✓ Remind your team: *"We don't work for God's love—we work from it."*
- ✓ Begin sets with a reminder of what Jesus has done.
- ✓ Let worship be your thank-you, not your transaction.

Devotional 35:
The Sound of Surrender

Scripture: *Romans 12:1 (NIV) -"Offer your bodies as a living sacrifice, holy and pleasing to God—this is your true and proper worship."*

Reflection:
The most powerful sound in worship isn't high notes—it's surrender. When a worshiper lays down pride, agenda, or preference at the feet of Jesus, that sound reaches heaven. Worship is not about *getting* something—it's about *giving* ourselves.
This is the kind of worship God desires—one where every note, every lyric, every expression flows from a surrendered heart.

Challenge:
Are you singing songs of surrender, or just songs with emotion?

Application:

- ✓ Take time to surrender your week, struggles, or agenda before rehearsals.
- ✓ Let one rehearsal be a full set of surrender songs and reflection.
- ✓ Regularly ask: *"What am I holding back from God?"*

Devotional 36: The Power of Unity in Worship

Scripture: Psalm 133:1 – *"How good and pleasant it is when God's people live together in unity!"*

Reflection:
Worship is not just about harmonizing voices—it's about harmonizing hearts. Unity is not uniformity; it is the supernatural ability to move together in spirit even when we're different in background, opinions, or personalities. A disunited worship team can play skillfully and still miss the anointing. The Holy Spirit flows through unity like oil flowing down Aaron's beard. When we come together in love, laying down ego and pride, our worship becomes a sweet fragrance that reaches heaven. True unity often requires sacrifice—of opinions, of preferences, and sometimes even of roles. But the reward is worth it: God commands His blessing there.

Challenge:
Are there unspoken tensions in the team? Are you carrying offense, jealousy, or silent judgment? Unity cannot coexist with secret strife.

Application:

- ✓ Set aside time this week to affirm and encourage a team member.
- ✓ During rehearsal, pray as a group for unity—especially before major services.
- ✓ Address unresolved issues with grace and honesty, always aiming to restore.

Devotional 37:
Worship from the Wilderness

Scripture: Habakkuk 3:17-18 – *"Though the fig tree does not bud… yet I will rejoice in the Lord…"*

Reflection:
It's easy to worship on the mountain when all is well, but true worship is forged in the wilderness. The heart that can sing even when dry is the one God treasures deeply. Every worship leader and team member will go through seasons of spiritual dryness, personal trial, or unanswered prayers. The wilderness teaches us to worship not because of the music, lights, or emotions—but because God is still worthy. Habakkuk teaches us that *rejoicing is a decision*, not a result of circumstances. As leaders of worship, we must model this resilience. We lead people into God's presence not because we're perfect, but because we know the way—even when it hurts.

Challenge:
Are you only worshiping when life is "working"? Or can you lead even when your own soul is in drought?

Application:

- ✓ Start your quiet time this week with thanksgiving—even if it's through tears.
- ✓ Share a brief testimony with the team about how you worshiped through a hard time.
- ✓ Remind yourself: you are not just leading songs—you're leading from scars, and that's powerful.

Devotional 38:
Excellence without Idolatry

Scripture: Colossians 3:23 – *"Whatever you do, work at it with all your heart, as working for the Lord, not for human masters."*

Reflection:

Excellence honors God. Sloppiness is not spiritual. But in our pursuit of excellence, we must guard against idolatry. Sometimes we begin with a desire to offer God our best, but it subtly shifts into perfectionism, pride, and performance. We start measuring our worth by applause, flawless delivery, or Instagram-worthy sets. But God sees beyond the performance—He sees the posture. Excellence is offering your best out of love, not fear. It's preparation with humility, not perfection for validation. If God is the audience, then our motivation changes. We tune our hearts before we tune our instruments.

Challenge:

Do you feel anxious or discouraged when a mistake happens? Do you crave validation from people more than from God?

Application:

- ✓ Ask yourself, "Would I prepare this well if no one ever complimented me?"
- ✓ Reflect on one area where excellence may have crossed into performance.
- ✓ Recenter your focus: excellence is worship, not self-worth.

Devotional 39: Guarding Your Anointing

Scripture: 2 Timothy 2:21 – *"If anyone cleanses himself... he will be a vessel for honor, sanctified and useful to the Master."*

Reflection:
The anointing is not about musical gifting—it's about spiritual depth. God doesn't anoint just any vessel; He anoints clean ones. We often focus on practicing harmonies, but forget to practice holiness. The sound may impress people, but only the anointing breaks chains. A worship team must be more than skilled musicians—it must be a consecrated priesthood. We're not called to be celebrities on stage, but servants in secret. Guarding your anointing means being careful with what you watch, speak, joke about, and dwell on. The Holy Spirit is sensitive, and His power flows freely through lives that are pure.

Challenge:
What private habit or compromise could be dulling your edge spiritually?

Application:

- ✓ Take a spiritual inventory this week: What needs to be laid down?
- ✓ Fast for a day to realign your heart and hear God more clearly.
- ✓ Start team meetings with a brief moment of personal repentance and renewal.

Devotional 40:
When God Says No

Scripture: 2 Corinthians 12:9 – *"My grace is sufficient for you, for my power is made perfect in weakness."*

Reflection:
There are times we pray for a breakthrough, for healing, or a door to open—and the answer is "No." As worshipers, how do we respond to divine silence or denial? Paul prayed three times for his thorn to be removed, and God didn't. Instead, God gave him grace and power. Our worship must be able to handle God's sovereignty. Mature worshipers don't just praise God for what He does—but for who He is, even when we don't understand His ways. God's "No" isn't rejection—it's redirection. Our stage may remain, but our attitude must mature.

Challenge:
Is your praise dependent on God's "yes"? Can you worship just as deeply when He says "wait" or "no"?

Application:

- ✓ Reflect this week on one area where God has said "no" or "not yet."
- ✓ Turn that place into a song of trust and surrender—write it out or journal it.
- ✓ Lead with authenticity, especially when sharing moments of disappointment and how God met you there.

Devotional 41: Private Devotion Before Public Display

Scripture: Matthew 6:6 – *"But when you pray, go into your room, close the door and pray to your Father…"*

Reflection:
Worship begins in secret. The most powerful public worship flows from deep private devotion. If we're only worshiping when people are watching, we've missed the point. Public worship without private prayer becomes performance. God wants to meet you on Monday morning, not just Sunday stage. Intimacy fuels authority. If your secret place is empty, your platform will eventually run dry. Worship leading is not about hyping a crowd—it's about carrying the presence of Someone you've met personally all week.

Challenge:
How's your personal altar? Do you meet with God when no one's looking?

Application:

- ✓ Set aside a daily 15-minute "secret place" with no phone, no agenda—just time with the Lord.
- ✓ Start team meetings with a moment of stillness to remind everyone of the private place.
- ✓ Model transparency—share what God is teaching you privately, not just your setlist.

Devotional 42:
Resting in God's Timing

Scripture: Ecclesiastes 3:1 – *"There is a time for everything, and a season for every activity under the heavens."*

Reflection:

In a fast-paced culture, we often confuse speed with success—even in ministry. But God works in seasons. Sometimes, you may feel overlooked on the team, underutilized, or sidelined. Other times, you may be in the spotlight but spiritually exhausted. Both are seasons. Trust God's timing. David was anointed as king, but went back to tending sheep. Jesus waited 30 years for a 3-year ministry. Rest is not laziness; it's obedience. Rushing ahead or forcing your way in ministry only leads to burnout or pride. Rest in His pace—He's preparing you.

Challenge:

Are you frustrated with your current role or pace in ministry?

Application:

- ✓ Write a prayer this week surrendering your timeline to God.
- ✓ Encourage another team member who may feel overlooked.
- ✓ Practice contentment—remind yourself that faithfulness in small things honors God.

Devotional 43: Leading with Love, Not Ego

Scripture: 1 Corinthians 13:1 – *"If I speak in the tongues of men and of angels, but have not love, I am a noisy gong…"*

Reflection:
Worship teams often involve gifting, leadership, and creative differences. But the moment ego enters, love exits. We can sing like angels but be noisy gongs in God's ears. True leadership is not about being heard, but about loving well. Love doesn't compete; it completes. Love prefers others, listens with humility, and builds up rather than shows off. Ego wants spotlight; love wants others to shine. Let's be known not just for our harmonies, but for how we honor one another.

Challenge:
Is there ego or comparison in your heart toward others on the team?

Application:

- ✓ Compliment someone's strength this week—especially someone you've compared yourself to.
- ✓ Lead with encouragement during rehearsal. Create a culture of honor.
- ✓ Evaluate your leadership moments: are they powered by love or self-importance?

Devotional 44:
Worship That Costs Something

Scripture: 2 Samuel 24:24 – *"I will not sacrifice to the Lord… that which cost me nothing."*

Reflection:
True worship always costs something. For David, it was money. For you, it might be time, energy, sleep, or comfort. Sacrifice is the soil where deep worship grows. We must be willing to show up early, stay late, practice when tired, and lead when discouraged. Worship that costs nothing is worth nothing. But when you lay something valuable down, God breathes on it. He sees the effort behind the excellence, the tears behind the melody, the prayers behind the harmony.

Challenge:
What is your worship costing you right now? Is it still sacrificial?

Application:

- ✓ Reflect: Am I giving God convenience or costly worship?
- ✓ Offer Him one thing this week that's inconvenient—but valuable.
- ✓ Remember: our greatest worship is our obedience, not our performance.

Devotional 45: Don't Miss the Moment

Scripture: *Luke 10:42* — "...Mary has chosen what is better, and it will not be taken away from her."

Reflection:
Martha was busy *serving* Jesus, but Mary was *sitting* at His feet. As worship leaders, it's easy to get so caught up in the execution of worship that we miss the encounter. Mary chose the better thing—not because service is wrong, but because intimacy must come first. What good is a flawless worship set if the team didn't meet Jesus in the process? Worship isn't about getting through the song list—it's about lingering at His feet. Sometimes the most spiritual thing we can do is to pause and adore.

Challenge:
Are you rushing through worship to reach the end—or resting to recognize Him?

Application:

- ✓ After your next worship session, take 5 minutes to remain in silence with the team. No words, just awe. Train your spirit to sit before you serve.

Devotional 46:
When the Sound Goes Silent

Scripture: *Habakkuk 3:17–18* — "Though the fig tree does not bud and there are no grapes on the vines… yet I will rejoice in the Lord, I will be joyful in God my Savior."

Reflection:
There are seasons in every worshiper's life where the music doesn't match the mood. The lights are dimmed, the instruments are ready, but your heart feels dry, silent, maybe even broken. Habakkuk faced a barren season—no fruit, no productivity, no evidence of God's blessing—yet he *chose* to rejoice. As worship leaders and musicians, we're often expected to overflow with joy and passion, but what do we do when we feel empty? Worship is not the overflow of circumstances; it is the overflow of a conviction that God is worthy, even when life isn't working. Worship isn't only what we do with instruments and microphones—it's our *decision* to anchor our voice in faith when feelings are absent. Sometimes the greatest worship happens when the sound stops—because that's when faith sings.

Challenge:
Are you only worshiping when things feel right? What do you do when you're leading others, but you're personally in a valley?

Application:

- ✓ Spend 10 minutes this week in silence before God—no instruments, no words, just waiting.

- ✓ Let your soul worship in stillness. Journal your raw emotions. Ask God to teach you to sing in silence.

Devotional 47:
The Invisible Audience

Scripture: *Matthew 6:4* — "...and your Father who sees in secret will reward you."

Reflection:
In our world of applause, likes, and public affirmation, worship can unintentionally become a performance. But Jesus reminds us that *God sees in secret*. The most powerful moments of worship don't happen on stage—they happen when no one is watching. True worshipers rehearse not just music but their *motives*. Are we moved more by God's presence than by people's applause? When we lead worship, we must be anchored by the awareness that our first audience is God, not the crowd. Public worship should be the overflow of private worship. If we have nothing secret with God, we may find ourselves performing rather than ministering. Let's cultivate depth behind the scenes so that what we do publicly is authentic.

Challenge:
Do you find more joy in being appreciated by others or being unseen by all but God?

Application:

- ✓ This week, choose one act of worship no one sees—write a personal song to God, pray alone, or worship in your room. Let it be raw and real. Remind yourself: *He sees*.

Devotional 48: No Substitutes for Sacrifice

Scripture: *Romans 12:1* — "...offer your bodies as a living sacrifice, holy and pleasing to God—this is your true and proper worship."

Reflection:
Many mistake talent for worship. A skilled musician can hit the notes, but it takes a surrendered heart to touch heaven. Paul tells us that real worship is sacrificial—offering ourselves. Not just our instruments, not just our voices—but our whole lives. In biblical times, a sacrifice meant something had to *die*. Worship will cost you. It might cost your pride, your time, your comfort, or your plans. But God is not after performance—He's after surrender. When we get on stage without personal surrender, we may inspire emotion but lack the weight of glory. Let worship cost you something. That's when it becomes fragrant to God.

Challenge:
Have you settled for musical excellence without personal surrender?

Application:

- ✓ Identify one area of your life that you need to lay on the altar. Commit it to God this week—your time, a habit, a desire. Worship with more than your hands—worship with your will.

Devotional 49:
Harmony Beyond the Chords

Scripture: *Psalm 133:1* — "How good and pleasant it is when God's people live together in unity!"

Reflection:
Musical harmony without *relational* harmony leads to noise in heaven's ears. A worship team can play the tightest set, but if there's division behind the scenes, the spiritual sound is off. God listens to hearts more than harmonies. Unity among the team creates a spiritual resonance that goes beyond music. When the team is humble, forgiving, and aligned, God commands a blessing. Worship is more than syncing instruments—it's syncing hearts. Before you tune your guitar, tune your relationships. The anointing flows where unity lives.

Challenge:
Are there hidden offenses or unresolved tensions among team members?

Application:

- ✓ Take initiative to reconcile this week. Send a message, make a call, or pray together.
- ✓ Do a heart check before every rehearsal—because your relationships affect your resonance.

Devotional 50:
From Gig to Glory

Scripture: *Colossians 3:23* — "Whatever you do, work at it with all your heart, as working for the Lord, not for human masters."

Reflection:
Worship ministry can start to feel like a job. Sound checks, schedules, planning meetings—it's easy to drift from calling to routine. When worship becomes a gig, we lose sight of the glory. Colossians reminds us: whatever we do, do it as unto the Lord. Every rehearsal is not just prep for Sunday—it's an offering to the King. Every chord, every lyric, every planning moment has eternal significance when done with the right heart. Let's never let the pressure of ministry rob us of the **joy of ministry**. Worship is not work—it's an honor.

Challenge:
Are you treating your role as a checklist or as a calling?

Application:
- ✓ Pause before your next team meeting or rehearsal. Say out loud: "This is for Your glory, Lord." Let that mindset shift the atmosphere.
- ✓ Worship begins *before* the set starts.

Devotional 51: Let the Lord Lead

Scripture: *2 Chronicles 20:21–22* — Jehoshaphat appointed singers to go *ahead* of the army, praising the Lord, and God set ambushes against their enemies.

Reflection:
In battle, logic says put the strongest up front. But in God's Kingdom, He often puts the *worshipers* at the frontlines. Worship isn't just a warm-up—it's warfare. When we lead in worship, we are going ahead of the people, creating a path for victory through praise. But here's the catch—we're not leading with our ideas. We must let *God* lead. Many worship teams struggle because they're chasing trends instead of the Spirit. Jehoshaphat didn't send the best musicians—he sent those who had hearts set on praise. The power came not from their music, but their obedience.

Challenge:
Are we letting the Spirit lead our sets—or our preferences?

Application:

- ✓ Pray together as a team before every set: "God, lead us, even if it interrupts our plan."
- ✓ Be sensitive to His prompting—even mid-song. Let worship be led from heaven.

Devotional 52:
The Posture of the Platform

Scripture: *Luke 18:14* — "For all those who exalt themselves will be humbled, and those who humble themselves will be exalted."

Reflection:
The platform is a dangerous place if our hearts are not anchored in humility. We can mistake being *used* by God for being *approved* by God. The Pharisee in Luke 18 prayed proudly—publicly. But Jesus honored the tax collector who bowed low. Worship is about **posture**—not just physical, but spiritual. You can raise your hands and still have a proud heart. God exalts those who worship low. Our platform must become a place of *humility*, not *visibility*. The true posture of a worshiper is bowed down, even when standing tall.

Challenge:
Are you seeking to be seen more than to serve?

Application:

- ✓ This week, kneel during your personal worship time—even if just for a few moments. Let your body reflect your humility. Ask God to keep your heart low even when you're high on the stage.

Crafting Your Own Worship Team Devotionals
A Worship Leader's Guide

As a worship leader, your influence goes beyond the platform. You are not only shaping the sound, but also shepherding the *spirit* of those who minister with you. Weekly devotionals are one of the most powerful tools to align the team's heart with God's purpose for worship. They provide rhythm, vision, depth, and spiritual calibration.

But what happens when the book ends?

You don't have to wait for someone else to write your next devotional—you can begin writing your own. This chapter is your practical and spiritual toolkit for creating meaningful, original devotionals that speak directly into the soul of your worship team.

Step 1: Begin in the Secret Place

"But Jesus often withdrew to lonely places and prayed." — Luke 5:16

Devotionals must be *born out of devotion.* Don't begin with a clever idea or a catchy title. Begin with prayer. Ask the Holy Spirit:

- ✓ "What does my team need this week?"
- ✓ "What is Your heart for us right now?"
- ✓ "What have You been speaking to me personally?"

The most powerful devotionals are *overflow*, not effort. They come from what God is already stirring in you.

Step 2: Listen for the Season

"To everything there is a season..." — Ecclesiastes 3:1

Every worship team has a spiritual *season*. Some are in seasons of transition, others of growth, healing, correction, or revival. Write devotionals that speak into the now. Ask:

- ✓ What challenges are surfacing among the team?
- ✓ Is there disunity, fatigue, or spiritual dryness?
- ✓ Are we facing pride, comparison, burnout, or complacency?

Write devotionals that bring clarity and courage to face the current moment.

Step 3: Choose One Worship-Centered Theme

Pick a single, **worship-focused lesson** per devotional. Here are some helpful starting points:

- ✓ The posture of the heart in worship
- ✓ Leading from brokenness
- ✓ Private worship vs public performance
- ✓ Holiness behind the sound
- ✓ Serving versus being seen
- ✓ Integrity in the unseen
- ✓ Obedience over talent
- ✓ Hosting God's presence

Let the focus be *narrow*. Don't try to teach too much in one devotional. One truth, deeply unpacked, transforms more than ten scattered thoughts.

Step 4: Anchor It in Scripture

"Your word is a lamp for my feet..." — Psalm 119:105

Find one key Scripture that clearly connects to the chosen theme. It doesn't have to be long, but it must be accurate and powerful. Read the passage in context. Ask:

- ✓ What truth does this verse teach about worship or the heart?
- ✓ What does this reveal about God's nature?
- ✓ What tension or challenge does it introduce?

Let Scripture be the foundation, not just a decoration.

Step 5: Write a Deep, Honest Reflection

This is where you pour out insight. In this section, reflect on:

- ✓ Why this truth matters for worship leaders/musicians
- ✓ What happens when we ignore or forget it
- ✓ What the Scripture reveals about God and worship
- ✓ A personal testimony or struggle related to the theme

Be vulnerable and real. Don't write like a preacher—write like a *shepherd*. This is where your team will feel seen, understood, and challenged.

✅ *Tip:* Aim for 2–3 paragraphs in this section. It should go deeper than surface encouragement—it should awaken conviction or vision.

Step 6: End with a Clear Challenge

This section helps turn revelation into responsibility. Ask:

- ✓ What decision or shift does this truth demand?
- ✓ What is God asking the team to lay down or pick up?
- ✓ How does this change the way we rehearse, lead, or live?

Keep the challenge *simple but direct*. You're calling them to respond—not just to think.

Step 7: Give a Practical Application

Always close with one **clear, actionable step** your team can take that week. Some examples:

- ✓ Spend 10 minutes in silent worship each day
- ✓ Reach out to a team member to reconcile
- ✓ Write a personal worship song from Psalm 23
- ✓ Kneel in worship privately before leading publicly
- ✓ Read Isaiah 6 and journal your response

Make sure the application is:

- ✓ Tangible
- ✓ Doable within the week
- ✓ Spiritually stretching

Step 8: Keep It Original and Spirit-Led

You don't need fancy words or poetic lines. What matters is authenticity and anointing. Write from your personal walk with God. Avoid copying popular devotionals. Your team doesn't need a polished piece—they need *a word in season*.

✨ *Reminder:* You don't have to be a writer. You just need to be *willing*.

Final Encouragement

God has trusted you with more than a team—He's trusted you with hearts. Your devotionals can set the tone for spiritual culture, relational health, and lasting fruit. As you lead worship on stage, let your written devotionals lead hearts into deeper places with Him off stage.

Write boldly. Write prayerfully. Write prophetically.

Because *sound without spirit is noise*—but worship born from truth and love is life-changing.

Worship Team Devotional Template

"Let the message of Christ dwell among you richly...through psalms, hymns, and songs from the Spirit." — Colossians 3:16

This template is structured to help you write devotionals that minister to the heart of worshipers and strengthen the spirit behind the sound. Use it weekly or as often as the Lord leads. Each section guides you to produce a well-rounded devotional with depth, challenge, and practical application.

---

1. Title

Choose a short, meaningful, and compelling title that captures the essence of the devotional. It should reflect the key lesson or theme.

Examples: "Worship in the Waiting" / "When the Lights Are Off" / "A Heart that Hosts"

---

2. Key Scripture

Pick one main Bible verse or short passage that supports and anchors the message.

Write out the verse (with reference)

Optional: Mention a few translations for richness of meaning

Example: "The Lord is near to the brokenhearted and saves the crushed in spirit." — Psalm 34:18 (ESV)

---

3. Reflection (2–3 Paragraphs)

This is the heart of your devotional. Unpack the Scripture and theme. Focus on how it relates to worship, the heart, attitude, or music ministry.

Include:

- ✓ A thoughtful, biblical reflection on the passage

- ✓ Why it matters for worship leaders/team members
- ✓ Real-life scenarios or personal insights
- ✓ Dangers of neglecting this truth
- ✓ How it relates to private devotion and public expression

Write from your walk. Don't preach—shepherd.

---

4. The Challenge (1 Paragraph)

This is where you present the *spiritual tension* or call to respond.

Ask:

- ✓ What is God inviting us to change, do, or become?
- ✓ What mindset needs to shift?
- ✓ What's at stake if we don't respond?

Write this in the form of a heartfelt nudge or prophetic invitation.

---

5. Application (1–2 Practical Steps)

Provide 1 or 2 simple, clear, and *doable* actions the team can take that week. These should help internalize and live out the devotional.

Ideas include:

- ✓ A short worship exercise or reflection
- ✓ A journal prompt or Scripture to meditate on
- ✓ A personal challenge (e.g., pray alone before rehearsal)
- ✓ A relational challenge (e.g., encourage a teammate)

The application should turn revelation into transformation.

---

6. Closing Prayer (Optional)
If you wish, end with a short, heartfelt prayer that seals the word. This can be read aloud together during team devotion time.
Keep it authentic and inviting the Holy Spirit.

☑ **Devotional Checklist**
Before using your devotional with the team, ask yourself:

- ✓ Is it rooted in Scripture?
- ✓ Is it relevant to worship or the heart behind it?
- ✓ Does it address a real challenge or growth area?
- ✓ Is it written from a place of prayer and authenticity?
- ✓ Is the application clear and achievable?
- ✓ Does it edify, correct, encourage, and align with God's Word?

Sample Mini Devotional Using the Template
Title: *"Unseen Worship"*
Scripture: *"Your Father who sees in secret will reward you." — Matthew 6:6*
Reflection:
Worship doesn't begin on stage—it begins in the secret place. Jesus reminded His disciples not to perform spirituality in public for the sake of appearances, but to develop intimacy with the Father behind closed doors. For worship leaders and musicians, the temptation to measure our worth by visibility is real. But the power of our public worship flows from the depth of our private surrender.
The Father sees what no one else does—the prayer behind the rehearsal, the tears during personal worship, the humility to yield a solo, the quiet

repentance after pride. These hidden offerings are what He honors. When we worship from a place that no one applauds but God, we create space for the *anointing* to flow, not just the sound.

Challenge:

Are we worshiping to be seen by others or to be known by God? Let's ask the Holy Spirit to purify our motives this week. Unseen worship is still powerful—and often more so.

Application:

- ✓ Spend 10 uninterrupted minutes each day this week in secret worship. No agenda, no songs—just surrender.
- ✓ Before rehearsal, pray aloud: *"God, this worship is for You alone. Purify my motives."*

About the Author
'GERARD ASSEY'

Gerard Assey is a Graduate in Economics, a PGD in Management (HRD) and holds a Doctorate in Leadership. Gerard holds several International Qualifications in Sales, Debt Collection, Training & Teaching, and is a 'Fellow' of the prestigious 'Institute of Sales & Marketing Management'-UK, a Certified NLP Practitioner, a 'Certified Trainer', an 'Accredited Management Teacher-Behavioral Sciences', a 'Certified Competency Facilitator', a 'Certified Management Consultant'- (the International credentials of a professional management consultant, awarded in accordance with global standards of the ICMCI); and a Certification from the University of Michigan in 'Successful Negotiation: Essential Strategies and Skills'

He is also a Member of the 'National Association of Sales Professionals' backed with several years experience in varied industries, both in India and Overseas. He also holds an 'Etiquette Consultant' Certification from the USA (by Sue Fox, Author of Best Seller: 'Business Etiquette for Dummies'. She has trained some of the top celebrities' world over). He was also a recipient of a scholarship for extensive training in Japan on 'Corporate Management for India'.

Gerard Assey is 'Founder & Chief Corporate Trainer' of the Group: '**Citius, Altius, Fortius Unlimited**'- an organization that **celebrated 20 years of Glorious Service** in 2021, focusing on 3 Core Competencies:

People. Performance. Profit; in functional areas of Sales & Marketing, HR & Organizational Development, covering Recruitment, Training & Consultancy!

Having managed organizations with large Sales Forces in India & Overseas, his specialization cover extensive areas of Sales Training (All levels - Presentation, Negotiation, Key/ Strategic Accounts Management & Managerial Skills for all sectors), Bid Proposal/ Capture Planning/ Management Trainings, Retail Sales, Customer Service & Customer Retention Programs, Training for Prevention & Collection of Debt, Self & Personal Development Programs (Time Management, Teamwork & Team Building, Business Etiquette & Personal Grooming, Leadership & Managerial Skills, People Management Skills, Train-the-Trainer etc), including preparation of Custom-designed Business Manuals for Internal (HR, Induction, and Sales etc) & External use (Instruction, User Manuals).

Gerard has successfully conducted over 6450 Trainings & Workshops (as of April '25) all across India, Middle East, Africa, Europe & S.E. Asia. Besides public programs conducted regularly, both in India & Overseas, he has some of the top names as clients whom he services from Single Owners to large Public & Government undertakings, covering all sectors, for their in-house needs.

His website: www.CollectionSkills.com is the only one in this part of the world to be featured in the 'Collections & Credit Risk Magazine-USA' under 'Who's Who in Training' and ranks TOP, along with other websites listed below on most search engines.

Gerard is author of 186 books already (April 2025), all the books being available on all online platforms and outlets as E-books and Paperbacks

A few of our business related books:

1. Bite-sized Bits on Commonsense Management
2. Heart to Heart on Life's Principles'
3. How to become a Successful Manager
4. The Sales Professionals' Master Workbook of S.Y.S.T.E.M.S
5. The Professional Business Email Etiquette Handbook & Guide
6. The Professional Business Video-Conferencing Etiquette Handbook & Guide
7. Professional Presentation Skills
8. Exceptional Customer Service
9. Professional Tele-Marketing Skills
10. Professional Debt Collection Skills
11. The G.R.E.A.T. Sales & Service Workbook
12. Sales Training Advantage for Results (*The Ultimate Sales Training Manual to enable you stand out as a S.T.A.R.*)
13. CEO Daily Planner & Organizer
14. The Sales Professionals' Master Daily Planner
15. The Professional Debt Collector's Master Daily Planner
16. My Daily Planner & Organizer
17. MY EMERGENCY INFORMATION RECORD (Family Emergency & Peace of Mind Planner)
18. The Ultimate Therapist & Counselors Planner and Organizer
19. Building an Ethical Workplace
20. Managing Relationships at Work
21. Managing Business Meetings Effectively
22. Effective Delegation Skills
23. Goal Setting for Success
24. B2B Selling by Email
25. Professional Business Etiquette & Grooming
26. Dining Etiquette & Table Manners
27. Effective Networking Skills
28. Grooming, Etiquette & Manners for Teens, Young Adults & Future Leaders
29. Inter-Personal Skills
30. Get Ready, Get Hired!
31. Selling in a Recession

32. Effective Receivables Management in an Economic Downturn!
33. Real Estate & Property Sales Training
34. Credit Sales & Accounts Receivable Management
35. Selling Skills for Real Estate & Property Advisors
36. Take G.R.E.A.T. C.A.R.E!
37. Spa, Salon & Health Club Selling Skills
38. Selling Travel, Holiday & MICE Services
39. Selling Skills for Spa's, Salons & Health Clubs
40. Retailing in Salons & Spas
41. Selling Holiday, Vacation, Tours & Packages
42. The Power of Sales Referrals
43. Selling Luxury
44. Technical Selling Skills
45. Financial Advisors Sales Training
46. Dealing with Burnout at Work Monopolize Your Markets
47. Selling to Affluent Customers
48. Growing up with Grace
49. Financial Selling Skills
50. *The Effective Manager's Guide: Key Skills to Thrive*
51. From Aspiring to Inspiring: A Guide for New Managers on the Rise
52. The Power of Focus
53. Selling with Integrity: Sell Like Jesus The Perfect Role Model!
54. 31 Habits of Champions: Your 31-Day Journey to Greatness
55. Rejecting Grasshopper Talk: From Grasshopper to Giant-Killer-*Defeating Giants Daily!*
56. Navigate the AI-Powered Future of Bid & Proposals: Up-Skill to Stay Relevant with Alternative Career Paths & Opportunities
57. Hiring Sales Winners
58. Present with Impact
59. Success Unlocked: *Breaking Free from Habits that Hold You Back*
60. Complaints to Cheers, Feedback to Gold: Mastering Complaints Management
61. Thriving Together: *Cultivating Diversity, Equity, and Inclusion*
62. Coaching Skills for Sales Managers

63. Soaring to Success in Business & Leadership: Swifter, Higher, Stronger!
64. From Classroom to Podium: A Student's Guide to Powerful Public Speaking & Presentation Skills
65. Developing Self-Discipline
66. The CEO's 31-Day Power Plan: Unlocking Success through Essential Traits
67. Credibility Matters
68. A Winning Attitude
69. Bid & Proposal Management Using AI
70. Sales Forecasting: A Practical & Proven Guide to Strategic Sales Forecasting
71. Elevate & Energize: *50 Dynamic & Fun Activities for Peak Workplace Morale*
72. 'Sales SOS! Sales on Fire! *30 Days to Conquer Chaos & the Nightmares of Success!'*
73. Mastering Sales Managerial Skills: *Building High-Performing Teams & Driving Exceptional Results*
74. Eagle-Eyed Leadership: Unleashing the Power of 31 Lessons from Eagles
75. The Ultimate Employee Training Guide: *Training Today, Leading Tomorrow*
76. Being More Accountable at Work
77. Creating a Culture of Continuous Improvement
78. Effective Questioning & Listening Skills
79. The Power of Value Selling
80. The Growth Mindset
81. Mastering Professional Help Desk Skills
82. The Power to Lead with Empathy
83. Being Prepared: The Key to Unlocking Success
84. Youthful Spark-Youth Energizers, Activities and Games-Igniting the Fun in Youth
85. Ignite your Motivation for Success
86. Elevate Your Executive Presence: *Your Roadmap to Executive Excellence*
87. Smart Decisions: *Mastering Problem Solving with Strategic Solutions for Business Success*
88. Strategic Planning: *Developing and Implementing Strategic Plans to Achieve Long-Term Business Goals*
89. The Power of Stay Interviews
90. Developing G.R.I.T.
91. Adaptability

92. Diagnosis- *A Key Skill for Leadership*
93. The Burnout-Proof Salesperson: *The Master Guide to Preventing Stress & Burnout-* Strategies for Thriving in Sales
94. Learning from Failure: *Keys to Success*
95. Customer Success Management
96. Overcoming the Killers of Motivation
97. The C-Suite Code: *Mastering Skills for Executive Excellence'*
98. Dealing with Difficult Customers
99. Unlocking Your Potential: Mastering the Top 20 Life Skills for a Brighter Future
100. Nurturing Tomorrow's Leaders: *Essential Soft Skills Every Child Must Learn*
101. Lively & Fun Party Games for Seniors & Elders
102. Role Playing for Sales Champions: From Practice to Performance
103. Fun and Exciting Party Games for Kids
104. Case Studies for Sales
105. Role-Playing for Unbeatable Customer Service
106. Case Studies in Customer Service
107. Case Studies in Winning Negotiations
108. Case Studies in Management & Leadership
109. Case Studies in Human Resources & Talent Management
110. CEO Success Blueprint: The Essential Toolkit for CEOs and C-Level Executives
111. The Salesperson's Self-Coaching Guide: *Master Your Own Self-Coaching Plan for Success*
112. Overcoming Procrastination: *Your Ultimate Guide to Stop Delaying and Start Living Your Best Life*
113. When True Colors Are Exposed: *The Journey to Unmasking Humanity*
114. Life-Changing Habits for Teens: Teen Success Blueprint for a Bright Future
115. Workplace Stress-Free: *Proven Strategies to Thrive at Work and Beyond*
116. Objection Overruled: *The Ultimate Guide to Turning 'No' into 'Yes'*

From the Ministry side, Gerard graduated in the very first batch of Charis Bible College-India & had for over 9 years served as a Part-time Faculty at Charis Bible College-Chennai (Andrew Wommack Ministries-Colorado, USA).
He is also a graduate of the Advanced Mentorship Program (AMP) and the Circle Of Ministerial Engagement (C.O.M.E.) of Prophet Jerome Fernando and a Spiritual Son of the Esteemed Prophet.
An accomplished author of several Secular & Christian Books, Gerard has been on the board of a few international organizations and boasts of being the SON of the MOST HIGH GOD: An ordinary guy following an extraordinary GOD!

...And some of his most recent Christian Books being:

1. A Bouquet of Praises for My KING
2. Christian Jokes for the Serious Religious' Folks!
3. Jesus Healed You!
4. Praise24Ever! (also in Tamil version)
5. The 5G Network of GOD
6. Building Faith over F.E.A.R- FACE EVERYTHING AND RISE with JESUS
7. Hebrew and Greek Praise and Worship Words
8. Godly Mothers' and Grandmothers' Bible Story time for Kids!
9. Miracles of Jesus in Pictures
10. Raise your Praise all 365 Days
11. Thanking GOD with an Attitude of Gratitude
12. Meditating on the Attributes of GOD
13. Puppet Scripts
14. Alcohol Ruins, JESUS Reforms, Renews & Restores!
15. Habakkuk 2:2 Christian Daily Journal, Planner & Organizer
16. ABC of GOD's Word for Handwriting Practice
17. Daily Bible Verse Handwriting Practice (Building Godly Character & Faith through Cursive Handwriting Practice!)
18. Guiding Light: Fun & Faith-Building Bible Activities for Children
19. Rejecting Grasshopper Talk: From Grasshopper to Giant-Killer-*Defeating Giants Daily!*
20. Teen Titans of Faith: *Building Courage, Determination & Christ-like-Esteem*
21. I AM Empowered: *Unleashing Divine Power with Positive Declarations*
22. Be A Solution Provider-*From Passion to Purpose*: *A Biblical Guide to Being the Answer to the World!*
23. Miracles of JESUS

24. Parables of Jesus for a Meaningful Life!
25. A Grateful Heart: Importance of Sharing Testimonies of GOD's Grace
26. Melodies of Worship to JESUS: 31 Songs of Praise & Worship From My Heart to HIS!
27. I AM SO BLESSED!
28. My Daily Cup of Energizer
29. 31 Leadership Lessons *from* Jesus- *The Supreme Leader*
30. Peace Amidst Storms: A Biblical Guide to Conquering S.T.R.E.S.S.
31. Rise Above: 20 Biblical Eagle Lessons for Life's Triumphs
32. Godly Goal Setting: *The FAITHFUL Blueprint for a Purpose-Driven Life*
33. The Profound Attributes of our Mighty GOD: Understanding the 10S's of the Almighty
34. Worship Now, Worship Forever: *A Journey from Earthly Praise to Eternal Glory*
35. Unceasing Praise & Worship: *365 Days to Worship the King*
36. The ROAR Within: *Living with Purpose and Authority through the Power of the Holy Spirit*
37. From Potential to Purpose: Unlocking and Multiplying Your Talents & Gifts for Kingdom Impact
38. Songs from the Heart: *Worshipping GOD in Your Own Tune & Melody*
39. Awakening Praise & Worship: Hebrew & Greek Words to Raise Your Praise
40. Sing a NEW Song to the LORD Everyday: *Daily Devotions of Praise & Worship to Lift Your Heart & Glorify HIS Name*
41. *The* A.R.O.M.A. of True Worship: *Creating Worship That Delights God*
42. Becoming A Kingdom Champion: *Embracing God's Call for a Life of Purpose & Victory*
43. The Busy Businessman's Daily Devotional: 366 Crisp Truths to Start Your Day Strong
44. The Teacher's Heart: *Daily Devotions for Educators*
45. Anchored! *A 31-Day Devotional for Students Facing Life's Challenges*
46. Suddenly! Unlocking Unorthodox Breakthroughs through Unusual Worship
47. Overcoming Adversity: *Lessons from the Bible for Modern Challenges*
48. LORD, Don't do it without me
49. Kingdom Leadership: *Biblical Principles for Modern Leaders*
50. Heartprints of God- *Growing God's Way:* Daily Devotions for Kids

to Shine Bright

51. Send Judah First: Let your Praises Go up First to See the Mighty Move of GOD
52. DIVINE MOMENTS: *Recognizing, Embracing, Preparing, and Walking into Life-Changing Encounters with God*
53. Be a Builder in the Kingdom: *The C.E.M.E.N.T. Guide to Creating a Lasting Legacy*
54. Unshakable: *Pillars of Godly Womanhood* (Pillars of Faith That Changed History)
55. Lead Like a Shepherd: *14 Essential Traits for Pastoral Excellence*
56. The Worship Leader's Arsenal: *Powerful Exhortations to Ignite Thanksgiving, Praise & Worship*
57. Women of UnShakable Faith: *31-Day Devotional for Strength, Purpose & Influence*
58. Called to Teach: *A Complete 10-Week Training Guide for Impactful VBS Teachers*
59. Strumming for the KING: Cowboy Songs of Faith & Fire
60. The Ultimate Youth Camp Playbook: *50 Bible-Centered Indoor Games to Engage, Equip, and Empower Teens*
61. Glad in HIS Presence: *David's Revelation of GOD's Love & Mercy*
62. The Spirit Behind the Sound: *52 Devotionals for Worship Teams*

Besides regularly contributing to business & trade journals, including international ones such as the 'Creative Training Techniques' and the 'Sales News' of the U.S.A, He is also a member of several prestigious bodies & trade associations, having participated in many Conferences & Workshops in India & Overseas.
Prior to his last assignment of leading & managing a large MNC as head, Gerard had a 3-year stint in the Middle East as a Consultant with a leading British Consultancy Firm.

As the past 'Official Country Representative' for the International Business Award- 'THE STEVIES'-(the business world's own Oscar) for about 4 years- he ensured a few Indian companies that qualify for the same every year!

Gerard can be contacted at:
Email: training@Sales-Training.in,training@CollectionSkills.com
Websites:
www.Sales-Training.in
www.EtiquetteWorks.in
www.CollectionSkills.com
www.RetailSalesTraining.in
www.SalesTrainingIndia.com
www.ManualPreparation.com
www.TrainingWithPuppets.com
www.FirstContactAcademy.com
www.SalesAndMarketingRecruiter.com

Our TRAININGS that can help your team

- ✓ **Sales Effectiveness**: Selling Skills for any Sector: Service/ Logistics/ FMCG Realty/ Insurance & Finance/ Media/ SPA's, Health Clubs & Salons/ Key Account Management, Effective Negotiation Skills/ Bid & Proposal Management Skills/ Retail Sales Training: Any Sector (Auto, Jewelry, Clothing, Luxury etc)
- ✓ **Customer Service Skills**-Complaints Handling & Customer Retention
- ✓ **Debt Prevention & Collection Skills**
- ✓ **Etiquette & Grooming**
- ✓ **Leadership & Managerial Skills**
- ✓ **Self & Personal Development Skills**: Presentation Skills/ Effective Communication Skills/Business Proposal Writing Skills/ Problem Solving & Decision Making Skills/ Empowering Secretaries-The perfect PA! (For Secretaries & PA's)/ Effective Time Management/ Teamwork & Teambuilding/ P.R.I.D.E- **P**ersonal **R**esponsibility **I**n **D**elivering **E**xcellence

www.ingramcontent.com/pod-product-compliance
Ingram Content Group UK Ltd.
Pitfield, Milton Keynes, MK11 3LW, UK
UKHW021341190726
13845UKWH00027B/661

9 788198 697400